Cognitive Psychology
Main Principles and Introduction to
Cognitive Behavior Therapy

Table of Contents

Chapter 1 Introduction to Cognitive Psychology

According to Oxford dictionary "Cognition" is "the mental action or process of acquiring knowledge and understanding through thought, experience, and the senses".

Cogito ergo sum is a Latin philosophical proposition by René Descartes usually translated into English as "**I think, therefore I am**".

Cognitive processes are continuously taking place in your mind and in the minds of the people around you. Whether you pay attention to a conversation, estimate the speed of an approaching car when crossing the street, or memorize information for a test at school, you are perceiving information, processing it, and remembering or thinking about it. We don't notice these processes considering them to be automatic and uncontrolled.

Chapter 2 Looking through your eyes

Have you ever been told that you "can't see something that's right under your nose"? How about that you "can't see the forest for the trees"? Have you ever listened to your favorite song over and over, trying to decipher the lyrics? In each of these situations, we call on the complex construct of perception. Perception is the set of processes by which we recognize, organize, and make sense of the sensations we receive from environmental stimuli (Goodale, 2000a, 2000b; Kosslyn & Osherson, 1995; Marr, 1982; Pomerantz, 2003). Perception encompasses many psychological phenomena. In this chapter, we focus primarily on visual perception. It is the most widely recognized and the most widely studied perceptual modality (i.e., system for a particular sense, such as touch or smell).

We do not perceive the world exactly as our eyes see it. Instead, our brain actively tries to make sense of the many stimuli that enter our eyes and fall on our retina. Depending on your viewpoint, objects can look quite different, revealing different details (look at any object, for example a chair, from 2 different positions). Thus, perception does not consist of just seeing what is being projected onto your retina; the process is much more complex. Your brain processes the visual stimuli, giving the stimuli meaning and interpreting them.

In his influential and controversial work, James Gibson (1966, 1979) provided a useful framework for studying perception. He introduced the concepts of distal (external) object, informational medium, proximal stimulation, and perceptual object.

Let's examine each of these.

The distal (far) object is the object in the external world (e.g., a falling tree). The event of the tree falling creates a pattern on an informational medium. The informational medium could be sound waves, as in the sound of the falling tree. The informational medium might also be reflected light, chemical molecules, or tactile information coming from the environment. For example, when the information from light waves come into contact with the appropriate sensory receptors of the eyes, proximal (near) stimulation occurs (i.e., the cells in your retina absorb the light waves). Perception occurs when a perceptual object (i.e., what you see) is created in you that reflects the properties of the external world. That is, an image of a falling tree is created on your retina that reflects the falling tree that is in front of you.

So, if a tree falls in the forest and no one is around to hear it, does it make a sound? It makes no perceived sound. But it does make a sound by creating sound waves. So the answer is "yes" or "no," depending on how you look at the question. "Yes" if you believe that the existence of sound waves is all that's needed to confirm the existence of a sound. But you would answer "no" if you believe the sound needs to be perceived (for the sound waves to have landed on the receptors in someone's ears). The question of where to draw the line between perception and cognition, or even between sensation and perception, arouses much debate with no ready resolution. Instead, to be more productive in moving toward answerable questions, we should view these processes as part of a continuum. Information flows through the system. Different processes address different questions. Questions of sensation focus on qualities of stimulation. Is that shade of red brighter than the red of an apple? Is the sound of that falling tree louder than the sound of thunder? How well do one person's impressions of colors or sounds match someone else's impressions of those same colors or sounds?

This same color or sound information answers different questions for perception. These are typically questions of identity and of form, pattern, and movement. Is that red thing an apple? Did I just hear a tree falling? Finally, cognition occurs as this information is used to serve further goals. Is that apple edible? Should I get out of this forest?

We never can experience through vision, hearing, taste, smell, or touch exactly the same set of stimulus properties we have experienced before. Every apple casts a somewhat different image on our retina; no falling tree sounds exactly like another; and even the faces of our relatives and friends look quite different, depending on whether they are smiling, enraged, or sad. Likewise, the voice of any person sounds somewhat different, depending on whether he or she is sick, out of breath, tired, happy, or sad. Therefore, one fundamental question for perception is "How do we achieve perceptual stability in the face of this utter instability at the level of sensory receptors?" Actually, given the nature of our sensory receptors, variation seems even necessary for perception! In the phenomenon of sensory adaptation, receptor cells adapt to constant stimulation by ceasing to fire until there is a change in stimulation. Through sensory adaptation, we may stop detecting the presence of a stimulus.

To study visual perception, scientists devised a way to create stabilized images. Such images do not move across the retina because they actually follow the eye movements. The use of this technique has confirmed the hypothesis that constant stimulation of the cells of the retina gives the impression that the image disappears (Ditchburn, 1980; Martinez-Conde, Macknik, & Hybel, 2004; Riggs et al., 1953).

The word "Ganzfeld" is German and means "complete field." It refers to an unstructured visual field (Metzger, 1930). When your eyes are exposed to a uniform field of stimulation (e.g., a red surface area without any shades, a clear blue sky, or dense fog), you will stop perceiving that stimulus after a few minutes and see just a gray field instead. This is because your eyes have adapted to the stimulus.

The mechanism of sensory adaptation ensures that sensory information is changing constantly. Because of the dulling effect of sensory adaptation in the retina (the receptor surface of the eye), our eyes constantly are making tiny rapid movements. These movements create constant changes in the location of the projected image inside the eye. Thus, stimulus variation is an essential attribute for perception.

There are different views on how we perceive the world. These views can be summarized as bottom-up theories and top-down theories. Bottom-up theories describe approaches where perception starts with the stimuli whose appearance you take in through your eye. You look out onto the cityscape, and perception happens when the light information is transported to your brain. Therefore, they are data driven (i.e., stimulus-driven) theories. Not all theorists focus on the sensory data of the perceptual stimulus. Many theorists prefer top-down theories, according to which perception is driven by high-level cognitive processes, existing knowledge, and the prior expectations that influence perception (Clark, 2003). These theories then work their way down to considering the sensory data, such as the perceptual stimulus. You perceive buildings as big in the background of the city scene because you know these buildings are far away and therefore must be bigger than they appear. From this viewpoint, expectations are important. When people expect to see something, they may see it even if it is not there or is no longer there. For example, suppose people expect to see a certain person in a certain location. They may think they see that person, even if they are actually seeing someone else who looks only vaguely similar (Simons, 1996). Top-down and bottom-up approaches have been applied to virtually every aspect of cognition. Bottom-up and top-down approaches usually are presented as being in opposition to each other. But to some extent, they deal with different aspects of the same phenomenon. Ultimately, a complete theory of perception will need to encompass both bottom-up and top-down processes.

Do we perceive objects in a viewer-centered or in an object-centered way? When we gaze at any object in the space around us, do we perceive it in relation to us rather than its actual structure, or do we perceive it in a more objective way that is independent of how it appears to us right this moment?

Right now one of your authors is looking at the computer on which he is typing this text. He depicts the results of what he sees as a mental representation. What form does this mental representation take? There are two common positions regarding the answer to this question.

One position, viewer-centered representation, is that the individual stores the way the object looks to him or her. Thus, what matters is the appearance of the object to the viewer (in this case, the appearance of the computer to the author), not the actual structure of the object. The shape of the object changes, depending on the angle from which we look at it. A number of views of the object are stored, and when we try to recognize an object, we have to rotate that object in our mind until it fits one of the stored images.

The second position, object-centered representation, is that the individual stores a representation of the object, independent of its appearance to the viewer. In this case, the shape of the object will stay stable across different orientations (McMullen & Farah, 1991). This stability can be achieved by means of establishing the major and minor axes of the object, which then serve as a basis for defining further properties of the object.

Both positions can account for how the author represents a given object and its parts. The key difference is in whether he represents the object and its parts in relation to him (viewer-centered) or in relation to the entirety of the object itself, independent of his own position (object-centered).

Consider, for example, the computer on which this text is being written. It has different parts: a screen, a keyboard, a mouse, and so forth. Suppose the author represents the computer in terms of viewer-centered representation. Then its various parts are stored in terms of their relation to him. He sees the screen as facing him at perhaps a 20-degree angle. He sees the keyboard facing him horizontally. He sees the mouse off to the right side and in front of him. Suppose, instead, that he uses an object-centered representation. Then he would see the screen at a 70-degree angle relative to the keyboard. And the mouse is directly to the right side of the keyboard, neither in front of it nor in back of it. One potential reconciliation of these two approaches to mental representation suggests that people may use both kinds of representations. According to this approach, recognition of objects occurs on a continuum (Burgund & Marsolek, 2000; Tarr, 2000; Tarr & Bülthoff, 1995). At one end of this continuum are cognitive mechanisms that are more viewpoint-centered. At the other end of the continuum are cognitive mechanisms that are more object-centered. For example, suppose you see a picture of a car that is inverted. How do you know it is a car? Object-centered mechanisms would recognize the object as a car, but viewpoint-centered mechanisms would recognize the car as inverted.

A third orientation in representation is landmark-centered. In landmark-centered representation, information is characterized by its relation to a well-known or prominent item. Imagine visiting a new city. Each day you leave your hotel and go on short trips. It is easy to imagine that you would represent the area you explore in relation to your hotel. Evidence indicates that, in the laboratory, participants can switch between these three strategies. There are, however, differences in brain activation among these strategies (Committeri et al., 2004).

Perceptual processes and change blindness play a significant role in accidents and efforts at accident prevention. About 50% of all collision accidents are a result of missing or delayed perception (Nakayama, 1978). Especially two-wheeled vehicles are often involved in "looked-but-failed-to-see" accidents, where the driver of the involved car states that he did indeed look in the direction of the cyclist, but failed to see the approaching motorcycle. It is possible that drivers develop a certain "scanning" strategy that they use in complex situations, such as at crossroads. The scanning strategy concentrates on the most common and dangerous threats but fails to recognize small deviations, or more uncommon objects like two-wheeled vehicles. In addition, people tend to fail to recognize new objects after blinking and saccades (fast movements of both eyes in one direction). Generally, people are not aware of the danger of change blindness and believe that they will be able to see all obstacles when looking in a particular direction ("change blindness blindness", Simons & Rensink, 2005; Davis et al., 2008).

This tendency has implications for the education of drivers with regard to their perceptual abilities. It also has implications for the design of traffic environments, which should be laid out in a way that facilitates complex traffic flow and makes drivers aware of unexpected obstacles, like bicycles (Galpin et al., 2009; Koustanai, Boloix, Van Elslande, & Bastien, 2008).

Chapter 3 Attention and Consciousness

Let's examine what it means to pay attention in an everyday situation. Imagine driving in rush hour, near a major sports stadium where an event is about to start. The streets are filled with cars, some of them honking. At some intersections the police are regulating the traffic, but not quite in synchrony with the traffic lights. This asynchronicity—with the traffic light signaling one thing and the police signaling another—divides your attention. Some cars are stranded in the middle of an intersection. Also, there are thousands of people streaming through the streets to attend the sports event. You need to pay close attention to the traffic light as well as the officer on the road, the cars passing by, and the pedestrians that might unexpectedly cross the street. What is it that lets us pay attention to so many different moving parts in traffic? What lets us shift attention if a pedestrian suddenly walks out into the street without notice? And why does our attention sometimes fail us, occasionally with drastic consequences such as a car accident?

> [Attention] is the taking possession of the mind, in clear and vivid form, of one out of what seem several simultaneously possible objects or trains of thoughts. … It implies withdrawal from some things in order to deal effectively with others.
>
> —William James, Principles of Psychology

It can be difficult to clearly describe in words what we mean when we talk about attention (or any other psychological phenomenon). So what do we refer to exactly, when we talk about attention in this chapter? Attention is the means by which we actively process a limited amount of information from the enormous amount of information available through our senses, our stored memories, and our other cognitive processes (De Weerd, 2003a; Rao, 2003). It includes both conscious and unconscious processes. In many cases, conscious processes are relatively easy to study. Unconscious processes are harder to study, simply because you are not conscious of them (Jacoby, Lindsay, & Toth, 1992; Merikle, 2000). For example, you always have a wealth of information available to you that you are not even aware of until you retrieve that information from your memory or shift your attention toward it. You probably can remember where you slept when you were ten years old or where you ate your breakfasts when you were 12. At any given time, you also have available a dazzling array of sensory information to which you just do not attend.

Whereas attention embraces all the information that an individual is manipulating (a portion of the information available from memory, sensation, and other cognitive processes), consciousness comprises only the narrower range of information that the individual is aware of manipulating. Attention allows us to use our limited active cognitive resources (e.g., because of the limits of working memory) judiciously, to respond quickly and accurately to interesting stimuli, and to remember salient information. Conscious awareness allows us to monitor our interactions with the environment, to link our past and present experiences and thereby sense a continuous thread of experience, and to control and plan for future actions. We actively can process information at the preconscious level without being aware of doing so. For example, researchers have studied the phenomenon of priming, in which a given stimulus increases the likelihood that a subsequent related (or identical) stimulus will be readily processed (e.g., retrieval from long-term memory). In contrast, in the tip-of-the-tongue phenomenon, another example of preconscious processing, retrieval of desired information from memory does not occur, despite an ability to retrieve related information.

Cognitive psychologists also observe distinctions in conscious versus preconscious attention by distinguishing between controlled and automatic processing in task performance. Controlled processes are relatively slow, sequential in nature, intentional (requiring effort), and under conscious control. Automatic processes are relatively fast, parallel in nature, and for the most part outside of conscious awareness. Actually, a continuum of processing appears to exist, from fully automatic to fully controlled processes. Two automatic processes that support our attentional system are habituation and dishabituation, which affect our responses to familiar versus novel stimuli.

One main function involved in attention is identifying important objects and events in the environment. Researchers use measures from signal-detection theory to determine an observer's sensitivity to targets in various tasks. For example, vigilance refers to a person's ability to attend to a field of stimulation over a prolonged period, usually with the stimulus to be detected occurring only infrequently. Whereas vigilance involves passively waiting for an event to occur, search involves actively seeking out a stimulus. People use selective attention to track one message and simultaneously to ignore others. Auditory selective attention (such as in the cocktail party problem) may be observed by asking participants to shadow information presented dichotically. Visual selective attention may be observed in tasks involving the Stroop effect. Attentional processes also are involved during divided attention, when people attempt to handle more than one task at once; generally, the simultaneous performance of more than one automatized task is easier to handle than the simultaneous performance of more than one controlled task. However, with practice, individuals appear to be capable of handling more than one controlled task at a time, even engaging in tasks requiring comprehension and decision making.

Some theories of attention involve an attentional filter or bottleneck, according to which information is selectively blocked out or attenuated as it passes from one level of processing to the next. Of the bottleneck theories, some suggest that the signal-blocking or signal-attenuating mechanism occurs just after sensation and prior to any perceptual processing; others propose a later mechanism, after at least some perceptual processing has occurred. Attentional-resource theories offer an alternative way of explaining attention; according to these theories, people have a fixed amount of attentional resources (perhaps modulated by sensory modalities) that they allocate according to the perceived task requirements. Resource theories and bottleneck theories actually may be complementary. In addition to these general theories of attention, some task-specific theories (e.g., feature-integration theory, guided-search theory, and similarity theory) have attempted to explain search phenomena in particular.

Early neuropsychological research led to the discovery of feature detectors, and subsequent work has explored other aspects of feature detection and integration processes that may be envolved in visual search. In addition, extensive research on attentional processes in the brain seems to suggest that the attentional system primarily involves two regions of the cortex, as well as the thalamus and some other subcortical structures; the attentional system also governs various specific processes that occur in many areas of the brain, particularly in the cerebral cortex. Attentional processes may be a result of heightened activation in some areas of the brain, of inhibited activity in other areas of the brain, or perhaps of some combination of activation and inhibition. Studies of responsivity to particular stimuli show that even when an individual is focused on a primary task and is not consciously aware of processing other stimuli, the brain of the individual automatically responds to infrequent, deviant stimuli (e.g., an odd tone). By using various approaches to the study of the brain (e.g., PET, ERP, lesion studies, and psychopharmacological studies), researchers are gaining insight into diverse aspects of the brain and also are able to use converging operations to begin to explain some of the phenomena they observe.

Chapter 4 Biological Hard Drive Disk – Memory

Memory is the means by which we retain and draw on our past experiences to use that information in the present (Tulving, 2000b; Tulving & Craik, 2000). As a process, memory refers to the dynamic mechanisms associated with storing, retaining, and retrieving information about past experience (Bjorklund, Schneider, & Hernández Blasi, 2003; Crowder, 1976). Specifically, cognitive psychologists have identified three common operations of memory: encoding, storage, and retrieval (Baddeley, 2002; Brebion, 2007; Brown & Craik, 2000). Each operation represents a stage in memory processing.
• In encoding, you transform sensory data into a form of mental representation.
• In storage, you keep encoded information in memory.
• In retrieval, you pull out or use information stored in memory.

Among the many tasks used by cognitive psychologists, some of the main ones have been tasks assessing explicit recall of information (e.g., free recall, serial recall, and cued recall) and tasks assessing explicit recognition of information. By comparing memory performance on these explicit tasks with performance on implicit tasks (e.g., word completion tasks), cognitive psychologists have found evidence of differing memory systems or processes governing each type of task.

Memory is the means by which we draw on our knowledge of the past to use this knowledge in the present. According to one model, memory is conceived as involving three stores: a sensory store is capable of holding relatively limited amounts of information for very brief periods; a short-term store is capable of holding small amounts of information for somewhat longer periods; and a long-term store is capable of storing large amounts of information virtually indefinitely. Within the sensory store, the iconic store refers to visual sensory memory.

One of memory model uses the concept of working memory, usually defined as being part of long-term memory and also comprising short-term memory. From this perspective, working memory holds only the most recently activated portion of long-term memory. It moves these activated elements into and out of short-term memory. A second model is the levels-of-processing framework, which hypothesizes distinctions in memory ability based on the degree to which items are elaborated during encoding. A third model is the multiple memory systems model, which posits not only a distinction between procedural memory and declarative (semantic) memory but also a distinction between semantic and episodic memory. In addition, psychologists have proposed other models for the structure of memory. They include a parallel distributed processing (PDP; connectionist) model. The PDP model incorporates the notions of working memory, semantic memory networks, spreading activation, priming, and parallel processing of information. Finally, many psychologists call for a complete change in the conceptualization of memory, focusing on memory functioning in the real world. This call leads to a shift in memory metaphors from the traditional storehouse to the more modern correspondence metaphor.

Among other findings, studies of mnemonists have shown the value of imagery in memory for concrete information. They also have demonstrated the importance of finding or forming meaningful connections among items to be remembered. The main forms of amnesia are anterograde amnesia, retrograde amnesia, and infantile amnesia. The last form of amnesia is qualitatively different from the other forms and occurs in everyone. Through the study of the memory function of people with each form of amnesia, it has been possible to differentiate various aspects of memory. These include long-term versus temporary forms of memory, procedural versus declarative memory processes, and explicit versus implicit memory. Although specific memory traces have not yet been identified, many of the specific structures involved in memory function have been located. To date, the subcortical structures involved in memory appear to include the hippocampus, the thalamus, the hypothalamus, and even the basal ganglia, and the cerebellum. The cortex also governs much of the long-term storage of declarative knowledge. The neurotransmitters serotonin and acetylcholine appear to be vital to memory function. Other physiological chemicals, structures, and processes also play important roles, although further investigation is required to identify these roles.

Chapter 6 Memory Processes

As mentioned in the previous chapter, cognitive psychologists generally refer to the main processes of memory as comprising three common operations: encoding, storage, and retrieval. Each one represents a stage in memory processing:
• Encoding refers to how you transform a physical, sensory input into a kind of representation that can be placed into memory.
• Storage refers to how you retain encoded information in memory.
• Retrieval refers to how you gain access to information stored in memory.
Our emphasis in discussing these processes will be on recall of verbal and pictorial material. Remember, however, that we have memories of other kinds of stimuli as well, such as odors (Herz & Engen, 1996; Olsson et al., 2009). Encoding, storage, and retrieval often are viewed as sequential stages. You first take in information. Then you hold it for a while. Later you pull it out. However, the processes interact with each other and are interdependent. For example, you may have found the Bransford and Johnson procedure difficult to encode, thereby also making it hard to store and to retrieve the information. However, a verbal label can facilitate encoding and hence storage and retrieval. Most people do much better with the passage if given its title, "Washing Clothes." Now, read the procedure again. Can you recall the steps described in the passage? The verbal label, "washing clothes" helps us to encode, and therefore to remember a passage that otherwise seems incomprehensible.

Encoding of information in short-term memory appears to be largely, although not exclusively, acoustic in form. Information in short-term memory is susceptible to acoustic confusability—that is, errors based on sounds of words. But there is some visual and semantic encoding of information in short-term memory. Information in long-term memory appears to be encoded primarily in a semantic form. Thus, confusions tend to be in terms of meanings rather than in terms of the sounds of words. In addition, some evidence points to the existence of visual encoding, as well as of acoustic encoding, in long-term storage. Transfer of information into long-term storage may be facilitated by several factors:
1. rehearsal of the information, particularly if the information is elaborated meaningfully;
2. organization, such as categorization of the information;
3. the use of mnemonic devices;
4. the use of external memory aids, such as writing lists or taking notes;
5. knowledge acquisition through distributed practice across various study sessions, rather than through massed practice.

However, the distribution of time during any given study session does not seem to affect transfer into long-term memory. The effects of distributed practice may be due to a hippocampal-based mechanism that results in rapid encoding of new information to be integrated with existing memory systems over time, perhaps during sleep. Studying retrieval from long-term memory is difficult due to problems of differentiating retrieval from other memory processes.

It also is difficult to differentiate accessibility from availability. Retrieval of information from short-term memory appears to be in the form of serial exhaustive processing. This implies that a person always sequentially checks all information on a list. Nevertheless, some data may be interpreted as allowing for the possibility of self-terminating serial processing and even of parallel processing.

Two of the main theories of forgetting in short-term memory are decay theory and interference theory. Interference theory distinguishes between retroactive interference and proactive interference. Assessing the effects of decay, while ruling out both interference and rehearsal effects, is much harder. However, some evidence of distinctive decay effects has been found. Interference also seems to influence longterm memory, at least during the period of consolidation. This period may continue for several years after the initial memorable experience.

Memory appears to be not only reconstructive—a reproduction of what was learned, based on recalled data and on inferences from only those data. It is also constructive—influenced by attitudes, subsequently acquired information, and schemas based on past knowledge. As shown by the effects of existing schemas on the construction of memory, schemas affect memory processes. However, so do other internal contextual factors, such as emotional intensity of a memorable experience, mood, and even state of consciousness. In addition, environmental context cues during encoding seem to affect later retrieval. Encoding specificity refers to the fact that what is recalled depends largely on what is encoded. How information is encoded at the time of learning will greatly affect how it is later recalled. One of the most effective means of enhancing recall is for the individual to generate meaningful cues for subsequent retrieval.

Chapter 7 Images inside your head

Ideally, cognitive psychologists would love to observe directly how each of us represents knowledge. It would be as if we could take a videotape or a series of snapshots of ongoing representations of knowledge in the human mind. Unfortunately, direct empirical methods for observing knowledge representations are not available at present. Also, such methods are unlikely to be available in the immediate future. When direct empirical methods are unavailable, several alternative methods remain. We can ask people to describe their own knowledge representations and knowledge representation processes: What do they see in their minds when they think of the Statue of Liberty, for example? Unfortunately, none of us has conscious access to our own knowledge-representation processes and self-reported information about these processes is highly unreliable (Pinker, 1985). Therefore, an introspectionist approach goes only so far.

Another possibility for observing how we represent knowledge in our minds is the rationalist approach. In this approach, we try to deduce logically how people represent knowledge. For centuries, philosophers have done exactly that. In classic epistemology—the study of the nature, origins, and limits of human knowledge—philosophers distinguished between two kinds of knowledge structures. The first type of knowledge structure is declarative knowledge. Declarative knowledge refers to facts that can be stated, such as the date of your birth, the name of your best friend, or the way a rabbit looks. Procedural knowledge refers to knowledge of procedures that can be implemented. Examples are the steps involved in tying your shoelaces, adding a column of numbers, or driving a car. The distinction is between knowing that and knowing how (Ryle, 1949). There are two main sources of empirical data on knowledge representation: standard laboratory experiments and neuropsychological studies. In experimental work, researchers indirectly study knowledge representation because they cannot look into people's minds directly. They observe how people handle various cognitive tasks that require the manipulation of mentally represented knowledge.

In neuropsychological studies, researchers typically use one of two methods: (1) they observe how the normal brain responds to various cognitive tasks involving knowledge representation, or (2) they observe the links between various deficits in knowledge representation and associated pathologies in the brain. In the following sections, we explore some of the theories researchers have proposed to explain how we represent and store knowledge in our minds:
• First, we consider what the difference is between images and words when they are used to represent ideas in the outside world, such as in a book.
• Then we learn about mental images and the idea that we store some of our knowledge in the form of images.
• Next, we explore the idea that knowledge is stored in the form of both words and images (dual-code theory).
• Finally, we consider an alternative—propositional theory—which suggests that we actually use an abstract form of knowledge encoding that makes use of neither words nor mental images.

Knowledge can be represented in different ways in your mind: It can be stored as a mental picture, or in words, or abstract propositions. In this chapter, we focus on the difference between those kinds of knowledge representation. Of course, cognitive psychologists chiefly are interested in our internal, mental representations of what we know. However, before we turn to our internal representations, let's look at external representations, like books. A book communicates ideas through words and pictures. How do external representations in words differ from such representations in pictures?

Some ideas are better and more easily represented in pictures, whereas others are better represented in words. For example, suppose someone asks you, "What is the shape of a chicken egg?" You may find drawing an egg easier than describing it. Many geometric shapes and concrete objects seem easier to represent in pictures rather than in words. However, what if someone asks you, "What is justice?"

Because symbols are arbitrary, their use requires the application of rules. For example, in forming words, the sounds or letters also must be sequenced according to rules (e.g., "c-a-t," not "a-c-t" or "t-c-a"). In forming sentences, the words also must be sequenced according to rules. For example, one can say "the cat is under the table," but not "table under cat the is."

Symbolic representations, such as the word cat, capture some kinds of information but not other kinds of information. The dictionary defines cat as "a carnivorous mammal (Felis catus) long domesticated as a pet and for catching rats and mice" (Merriam-Webster's Online Dictionary, 2010). Suppose our own mental representations for the meanings of words resemble those of the dictionary. Then the word cat connotes an animal that eats meat ("carnivorous"), nurses its young
("mammal"), and so on. This information is abstract and general. It may be applied to any number of specific cats having any fur color or pattern. To represent additional characteristics, we must use additional words, such as black, Persian, or calico.

Pictures and words also represent relationships in different ways. To summarize, pictures aptly capture concrete and spatial information in a manner analogous to whatever they represent. They convey all features simultaneously. In general, any rules for creating or understanding pictures pertain to the analogous relationship between the picture and what it represents. They help ensure as much similarity as possible between the picture and the object it represents. Words, on the contrary, handily capture abstract and categorical information in a manner that is symbolic of whatever the words represent. Representations in words usually convey information sequentially. They do so according to arbitrary rules that have little to do with what the words represent. Pictures and words are both well suited to some purposes but not to others. For example, blueprints and identification photos serve different purposes than essays and memos. Now that we have some preliminary ideas about external representations of knowledge, let's consider internal representations of knowledge. Specifically, how do we represent what we know in our minds? Do we have mental scenarios (pictures) and mental narratives (words)?

Knowledge representation comprises the various ways in which our minds create and modify mental structures that stand for what we know about the world outside our minds. Knowledge representation involves both declarative (knowing that) and nondeclarative (knowing how) forms of knowledge. Through mental imagery, we create analog mental structures that stand for things that are not presently being sensed in the sense organs. Imagery may involve any of the senses, but the form of imagery most commonly reported by laypeople and most commonly studied by cognitive psychologists is visual imagery. Some studies (e.g., studies of blind participants and some studies of the brain) suggest that visual imagery itself may comprise two discrete systems of mental representation: One system involves nonspatial visual attributes, such as color and shape; another involves spatial attributes, such as location, orientation, and size or distance scaling. According to Paivio's dual-code hypothesis, two discrete mental codes for representing knowledge exist. One code is for images and another for words and other symbols. Images are represented in a form analogous to the form we perceive through our senses. In contrast, words and concepts are encoded in a symbolic form, which is not analogical. An alternative view of image representation is the propositional hypothesis. It suggests that both images and words are represented in a propositional form. The proposition retains the underlying meaning of either images or words, without any of the perceptual features of either. For example, the acoustic features of the sounds of the words are not stored, nor are the visual features of the colors or shapes of the images. Furthermore, propositional codes, more than imaginal codes, seem to influence mental representation when participants are shown ambiguous or abstract figures. Apparently, unless the context facilitates performance, the use of visual images does not always readily lead to successful performance on some tasks requiring mental manipulations of either abstract figures or ambiguous figures.

Based on a modification of the dualcode view, Shepard and others have espoused a functional-equivalence hypothesis. It asserts that images are represented in a form functionally equivalent to percepts, even if the images are not truly identical to percepts. Studies of mental rotations, image scaling, and image scanning suggest that imaginal task performance is functionally equivalent to perceptual task performance. Even performance on some tasks involving comparisons of auditory images seems to be functionally equivalent to performance on tasks involving comparisons of auditory percepts. Propositional codes seem less likely to influence mental representation than imaginal ones when participants are given an opportunity to create their own mental images. For example, they might do so in tasks involving image sizing or mental combinations of imaginal letters. Some researchers have suggested that experimenter expectancies may have influenced cognitive studies of imagery, but others have refuted these suggestions. In any case, neuropsychological studies are not subject to such influences. They seem to support the functional equivalence hypothesis by finding overlapping brain areas involved in visual perception and mental rotation.

Kosslyn has synthesized these various hypotheses to suggest that images may involve both analogous and propositional forms of knowledge representation. In this case, both forms influence our mental representation and manipulation of images. Thus, some of what we know about images is represented in a form that is analogous to perception. Other things we know about images are represented in a propositional form.

Johnson-Laird has proposed an alternative synthesis. He has suggested that knowledge may be represented as verbally expressible propositions, as somewhat abstracted analogical mental models, or as highly concrete and analogical mental images. Studies of split-brain patients and patients with lesions indicate some tendency toward hemispheric specialization. Visuospatial information may be processed primarily in the right hemisphere. Linguistic (symbolic) information may be processed primarily in the left hemisphere of right-handed individuals. A case study suggests that spatial imagery also may be processed in a different region of the brain than the regions in which other aspects of visual imagery are processed. Studies of normal participants show that visual-perception tasks seem to involve regions of the brain similar to the regions involved in visual-imagery tasks.

People tend to distort their own mental maps in ways that regularize many features of the maps. For example, they may tend to imagine right angles, symmetrical forms, either vertical or horizontal boundaries (not oblique ones), and well-aligned figures and objects. People also tend to employ distortions of their mental maps in ways that support their propositional knowledge about various landmarks. They tend to cluster similar landmarks, to segregate dissimilar ones, and to modify relative positions to agree with conceptual knowledge about the landmarks. In addition, people tend to distort their mental maps. They increase their estimates regarding the distances between endpoints as the density of intervening landmarks increases. Some of the heuristics that affect cognitive maps support the notion that propositional information influences imaginal representations. The influence of propositional information may be particularly potent when participants are not shown a graphic map. Instead, they are asked to read a narrative passage and to envision themselves as participants in a setting described in the narrative.

Chapter 8 Language

I stood still, my whole attention fixed upon the motions of her fingers. Suddenly,
I felt a misty consciousness as of something forgotten—a thrill of returning
thought; and somehow the mystery of language was revealed to me.
I knew then that "w-a-t-e-r" meant the wonderful cool something that was flowing over my hand. That living word awakened my soul, gave it
light, joy, set it free! ... Everything had a name, and each name gave birth to a new thought. As we returned to the house every object which
I touched seemed to quiver with life.... I learned a great many new words that day ... words that were to make the world blossom for me.
—Helen Keller, Story of My Life

Helen Keller became both blind and deaf at 19 months of age after a severe childhood illness. She was first awakened to a sentient, thought-filled, comprehensible world through her teacher, Anne Sullivan. The miracle worker held one of Helen's hands under a spigot from which a stream of water gushed over Helen's hand. All the while she spelled with a manual alphabet into Helen's other hand the mind awakening word "w-a-t-e-r." Language is the use of an organized means of combining words in order to communicate with those around us. It also makes it possible to think about things and processes we currently cannot see, hear, feel, touch, or smell. These things include ideas that may not have any tangible form. As Helen Keller demonstrated, the words we use may be written, spoken, or otherwise signed (e.g., via American Sign Language [ASL]). Even so, not all communication—exchange of thoughts and feelings—is through language. Communication encompasses other aspects—nonverbal communication, such as gestures or facial expressions, can be used to embellish or to indicate. Glances may serve many purposes. For example, sometimes they are deadly, other times, seductive. Communication can also include touches, such as handshakes, hits, and hugs. These are only a few of the means by which we can communicate. Psycholinguistics is the psychology of our language as it interacts with the human mind. It considers both production and comprehension of language (Gernsbacher & Kaschak, 2003a, 2003b; Wheeldon, Meyer, & Smith, 2003). Four areas of study have contributed greatly to an understanding of psycholinguistics:
• linguistics, the study of language structure and change;
• neurolinguistics, the study of the relationships among the brain, cognition, and language;
• sociolinguistics, the study of the relationship between social behavior and language (Carroll, 1986); and
• computational linguistics and psycholinguistics, the study of language via computational methods (Coleman, 2003; Gasser, 2003; Lewis, 2003).

There are almost 7,000 languages spoken in the world today (Lewis, 2009). New Guinea is the country with the most languages in the world—it has more than 850 indigenous languages, which means that on average, each language has just about 7,000 speakers. Surprisingly, there are still languages today that have not even been "discovered" and named by scientists. A linguist who traveled to southwestern China's Yunnan province in 2006 discovered 18 languages, spoken by members of the Phula ethnic group, that never before had been defined and named (Erard, 2009). It is to be expected that there are many more languages that linguists do not yet know about. Part of the reason for the Phula languages' not having been discovered earlier is that speakers of the language live in mountainous areas that are hard to access. What exactly constitutes a language, and are there some things that all languages have in common?

Languages can be strikingly different, but they all have some commonalities (Brown, 1965; Clark & Clark, 1977; Glucksberg & Danks, 1975). No matter what language you speak, language is:

1. communicative: Language permits us to communicate with one or more people who share our language.
2. arbitrarily symbolic: Language creates an arbitrary relationship between a symbol and what it represents: an idea, a thing, a process, a relationship, or a description.
3. regularly structured: Language has a structure; only particularly patterned arrangements of symbols have meaning, and different arrangements yield different meanings.
4. structured at multiple levels: The structure of language can be analyzed at more than one level (e.g., in sounds, meaning units, words, and phrases).
5. generative, productive: Within the limits of a linguistic structure, language users can produce novel utterances. The possibilities for creating new utterances are virtually limitless.
6. dynamic: Languages constantly evolve.

Let's examine the six properties of language in more detail. The communicative property of language may be the most obvious feature, but it is also the most remarkable one. As an example, you can write what you are thinking and feeling so that others may read and understand your thoughts and feelings. Yet, as you may know from your own experience, there are occasional flaws in the communicative property of language. Despite the frustrations of miscommunications, however, for one person to be able to use language to communicate to another is impressive. What may be more surprising is the second property of language. We communicate through our shared system of arbitrary symbolic reference to things, ideas, processes, relationships, and descriptions (Steedman, 2003).

Words are symbols that were chosen arbitrarily to represent something else, such as a "tree," "swim," or "brilliant." The thing or concept in the real world that a word refers to is called referent. By consensual agreement, these combinations of letters or sounds may be meaningful to us. But the particular symbols themselves do not lead to the meaning of the word, which is why different languages use very different sounds to refer to the same thing. Symbols are convenient because we can use them to refer to things, ideas, processes, relationships, and descriptions that are not currently present, such as the Amazon River. We even can use symbols to refer to things that never have existed, such as dragons or elves. And we can use symbols to refer to things that exist in a form that is not physically tangible, such as calculus, truth, or justice. Without arbitrary symbolic reference, we would be limited to symbols that somehow resembled the things they are symbolizing (e.g., we would need a treelike symbol to represent a tree).

Two principles underlying word meanings are the principle of conventionality and the principle of contrast (Clark, 1993, 1995; Diesendruck, 2005). The principle of conventionality simply states that meanings of words are determined by conventions—they have a meaning upon which people agree. According to the principle of contrast, different words have different meanings. Thus, when you have two different words, they represent two things that are at least slightly different. Otherwise, what would be the point of having two different words for the same thing?

The third property is the regular structure of language: Particular patterns of sounds and of letters form meaningful words. Random sounds and letters, however, usually do not. Furthermore, particular patterns of words form meaningful sentences, paragraphs, and discourse. Most others make no sense.

The fourth property is that language is structured at multiple levels. Any meaningful utterance can be analyzed at more than one level. Let's see at what levels psycholinguists study language. They look at:
• sounds, such as p and t;

• words, such as "pat," "tap," "pot," "top," "pit," and "tip;"
• sentences, such as "Pat said to tap the top of the pot, then tip it into the pit;" and
• larger units of language, such as this paragraph or even this book.

A fifth property of language is productivity (sometimes termed generativity). Productivity refers here to our vast ability to produce language creatively. However, our use of language does have limitations. We have to conform to a particular structure and use a shared system of arbitrary symbols. We can use language to produce an infinite number of unique sentences and other meaningful combinations of words. Although the number of sounds (e.g., s as in "hiss") used in a language may be finite, the various sounds can be combined endlessly to form new words and new sentences. Among them are many novel utterances—linguistic expressions that are brand new and have never been spoken before by anyone. Thus, language is inherently creative. None of us possibly could have heard previously all the sentences we are capable of producing and that we actually produce in the course of our everyday lives. Any language appears to have the potential to express any idea in it that can be expressed in any other language. However, the ease, clarity, and succinctness of expression of a particular idea may vary greatly from one language to the next. Thus, the creative potential of different languages appears to be roughly the same.

Finally, the productive aspect of language quite naturally leads to the dynamic, evolutionary nature of language. Individual language users coin words and phrases and modify language usage. The wider group of language users either accepts or rejects the modifications. Each year, recently coined words are added to the dictionary, signifying the extensive acceptance of these new words. For example, you may be familiar with the words netiquette (a blend of "network" and "etiquette," referring to appropriate behavior on-line), emoticon (a blend of "emotion" and "icon," referring to punctuation symbols used in emails to indicate emotions), and webinar (referring to a seminar held on-line). All of these words have been created just in recent years. Can you think of other newly minted words that did not exist a decade ago? Similarly, words that are no longer used are removed from the dictionary, further contributing to the evolution of language. To imagine that language would never change is almost as incomprehensible as to imagine that people and environments would never change. For example, the modern English we speak now evolved from Middle English, and Middle English evolved from Old English.

Have you ever needed to communicate with someone over the phone, but the speech you heard was garbled because of faulty cell phone reception? If so, you will agree that speech perception is fundamental to language use in our everyday lives. Understanding speech is crucial to human communication. In this section, we investigate how we perceive speech. We also reflect on the question of whether speech is somehow special among all the various sounds we can perceive. We are able to perceive speech with amazing rapidity. On the one hand, we can perceive as many as fifty phonemes per second in a language in which we are fluent (Foulke & Sticht, 1969). When confronted with non-speech sounds, on the other hand, we can perceive less than one phone per second (Warren et al., 1969). This limitation explains why foreign languages are difficult to understand (when we hear them), and sound like they are spoken quickly. The sounds of their letters and letter combinations are different from the sounds corresponding to the same letters and letter combinations in our native language. For example, the author's Spanish sounds "American" because he tends to reinterpret Spanish sounds in terms of the American English phonetic system, rather than the Spanish one. Another problem we face when we try to understand what somebody else is saying is that no word sounds exactly the same when it is spoken across the various speakers who say the word. There is a lot of variability across people in the pronunciation of words. People speak faster or slower, or they may pronounce sounds differently depending on where they come from. For example, one of the author's elementary school teachers pronounced "get" in a way that sounded like "git." Speech sounds are very variable, but even if a word sounds different every time we hear it, we still need to be able to figure out what word it is. What makes it even more complicated is that often we pronounce more than one sound at the same time. This is called coarticulation. One or more phonemes begin while other phonemes still are being produced. For example, say the words "palace" and "pool." They both begin with a p sound. But can you notice a difference in the shape of your lips when you say the p of "pool" as compared to the p of "palace"? You are already preparing for the following vowel as you pronounce the p sound, and this impacts the sound you produce. Not only do phonemes within a word overlap, but the boundaries between words in continuous speech also tend to overlap. Coarticulation can be observed in nonverbal language as well. A number of studies have been completed that examine speech production in skilled signers (i.e., people who communicate in sign language). People who are skilled signers can convey many paragraphs worth of information in less than a minute (Lupton, 1998). A great deal of coarticulation occurs in skilled use of American Sign Language (ASL) (Grosvald & Corina, 2008; Jerde, Soechting, & Flanders, 2003). This coarticulation affects a number of aspects of the sign, both as it begins and as it leads into another sign. The affected aspects include hand shape, movement, and position (Yang & Sarkar, 2006). Coarticulation occurs more frequently with more informal forms of ASL (Emmorey, 1994). People who are just learning sign language are more likely to use the more formal form. Later, as people become more skillful, they typically begin to use the more informal forms. Therefore, as skill and fluency increase, so does the incidence of coarticulation. Coarticulation is a result of the anticipation of the next sign, much in the same way that verbal coarticulation is based on the anticipation of the next word. This coarticulation does not, however, typically impair understanding. These observations support the unique nature of language perception, regardless of whether its format is spoken or signed.

There are at least six properties of language, defined as the use of an organized means of combining words in order to communicate. (1) Language permits us to communicate with one or more people who share our language. (2) Language creates an arbitrary relationship between a symbol and its referent—an idea, a thing, a process, a relationship, or a description. (3) Language has a regular structure; only particular sequences of symbols (sounds and words) have meaning. Different sequences yield different meanings. (4) The structure of language can be analyzed at multiple levels (e.g., phonemic and morphemic). (5) Despite having the limits of a structure, language users can produce novel utterances; the possibilities for generating new utterances are virtually limitless. (6) Languages constantly evolve. Language involves verbal comprehension—the ability to comprehend written and spoken linguistic input, such as words, sentences, and paragraphs. It also involves verbal fluency—the ability to produce linguistic output. The smallest units of sound produced by the human vocal tract are phones. Phonemes are the smallest units of sound that can be used to differentiate meaning in a given language. The smallest semantically meaningful unit in a language is a morpheme. Morphemes may be either roots or affixes—prefixes or suffixes. Affixes in turn may be either content morphemes, conveying the bulk of the word's meaning, or function morphemes, augmenting the meaning of the word. A lexicon is the repertoire of morphemes in a given language (or for a given language user). The study of the meaningful sequencing of words within phrases and sentences in a given language is syntax. Larger units of language are embraced by the study of discourse.

In speech perception, listeners must overcome the influence of coarticulation (overlapping) of phonemes on the acoustic structure of the speech signal. Categorical perception is the phenomenon in which listeners perceive continuously varying speech sounds as distinct categories. It lends support to the notion that speech is perceived via specialized processes. The motor theory of speech perception attempts to explain these processes in relation to the processes involved in speech production. Those who believe speech perception is ordinary explain speech perception in terms of feature-detection, prototype, and Gestalt theories of perception. Syntax is the study of the linguistic structure of sentences. Phrase-structure grammars analyze sentences in terms of the hierarchical relationships among words in phrases and sentences. Transformational grammars analyze sentences in terms of transformational rules that describe interrelationships among the structures of various sentences. Some linguists have suggested a mechanism for linking syntax to semantics. By this mechanism, grammatical sentences contain particular slots for syntactical categories. These slots may be filled by words that have particular thematic roles within the sentences. According to this view, each item in a lexicon contains information regarding appropriate thematic roles, as well as appropriate syntactical categories.

The reading difficulties of people with dyslexia often relate to problems with the perceptual aspects of reading. Reading comprises two basic kinds of processes: (1) lexical processes, which include sequences of eye fixations and lexical access; and (2) comprehension processes.

Obviously, we can understand discourse only through analysis of words. But sometimes we understand words through discourse. For one example, sometimes in a conversation or watching a movie, we miss a word. The context of the discourse helps us figure out what the word was likely to be. As a second example, sometimes a word can have several meanings, such as "well." We use discourse to help us figure out which meaning is intended. As a third example, sometimes we realize, through discourse, that a word is intended to mean something different from its actual meaning, as in "Yeah, right!" Here, "right" is likely to be intended to mean "not really right at all." So discourse helps us understand individual words, just as the individual words help us understand discourse.

Chapter 9 Considering

Early theories were designed to achieve practical mathematical models of decision making and assumed that decision makers are fully informed, infinitely sensitive to information, and completely rational. Subsequent theories began to acknowledge that humans often use subjective criteria for decision making, that chance elements often influence the outcomes of decisions, that humans often use subjective estimates for considering the outcomes, and that humans are not boundlessly rational in making decisions. People apparently often use satisficing strategies, settling for the first minimally acceptable option, and strategies involving a process of elimination by aspects to eliminate an overabundance of options. One of the most common heuristics most of us use is the representativeness heuristic. We fall prey to the fallacious belief that small samples of a population resemble the whole population in all respects. Our misunderstanding of base rates and other aspects of probability often leads us to other mental shortcuts as well, such as in the conjunction fallacy and the inclusion fallacy.

Another common heuristic is the availability heuristic, in which we make judgments based on information that is readily available in memory, without bothering to seek less available information. The use of heuristics, such as anchoring and adjustment, illusory correlation, and framing effects, also often impairs our ability to make effective decisions. Once we have made a decision (or better yet, another person has made a decision) and the outcome of the decision is known, we may engage in hindsight bias, skewing our perception of the earlier evidence in light of the eventual outcome. Perhaps the most serious of our mental biases, however, is overconfidence, which seems to be amazingly resistant to evidence of our own errors.

Deductive reasoning involves reaching conclusions from a set of conditional propositions or from a syllogistic pair of premises. Among the various types of syllogisms are linear syllogisms and categorical syllogisms. In addition, deductive reasoning may involve complex transitive inference problems or mathematical or logical proofs involving large numbers of terms. Also, deductive reasoning may involve the use of pragmatic reasoning schemas in practical, everyday situations. In drawing conclusions from conditional propositions, people readily apply the modus ponens argument, particularly regarding universal affirmative propositions. Most of us have more difficulty, however, in using the modus tollens argument and in avoiding deductive fallacies, such as affirming the consequent or denying the antecedent, particularly when faced with propositions involving particular propositions or negative propositions. In solving syllogisms, we have similar difficulties with particular premises and negative premises and with terms that are not presented in the customary sequence. Frequently, when trying to draw conclusions, we overextend a strategy from a situation in which it leads to a deductively valid conclusion to one in which it leads to a deductive fallacy. We also may foreclose on a given conclusion before considering the full range of possibilities that may affect the conclusion. These mental shortcuts may be exacerbated by situations in which we engage in confirmation bias (tending to confirm our own beliefs). We can enhance our ability to draw well reasoned conclusions in many ways, such as by taking time to evaluate the premises or propositions carefully and by forming multiple mental models of the propositions and their relationships. We also may benefit from training and practice in effective deductive reasoning. We are particularly likely to reach well-reasoned conclusions when such conclusions seem plausible and useful in pragmatic contexts, such as during social exchanges.

Although we cannot reach logically certain conclusions through inductive reasoning, we can at least reach highly probable conclusions through careful reasoning. When making categorical inferences, people tend to use both top-down and bottom-up strategies. Processes of inductive reasoning generally form the basis of scientific study and hypothesis testing as a means to derive causal inferences. In addition, in reasoning by analogy people often spend more time encoding the terms of the problem than in performing the inductive reasoning. Reasoning by analogy can lead to better conclusions, but also to worse ones if the analogy is weak or based on faulty assumptions. It appears that people sometimes may use reasoning based on formal rule systems, such as by applying rules of formal logic, and sometimes use reasoning based on associations, such as by noticing similarities and temporal contiguities.

A number of scientists have suggested that people have two distinct systems of reasoning: an associative system that is sensitive to observed similarities and temporal contiguities and a rule-based system that involves manipulations based on relations among symbols. The two systems can work together to help us reach reasonable conclusions in an efficient way.

Problem solving involves mentally working to overcome obstacles that stand in the way of reaching a goal. The key steps of problem solving are problem identification, problem definition and representation, strategy construction, organization of information, allocation of resources, monitoring, and evaluation. In everyday experiences, these steps may be implemented very flexibly. Various steps may be repeated, may occur out of sequence, or may be implemented interactively.

Although well-structured problems may have clear paths to solution, the route to solution still may be difficult to follow. Some well-structured problems can be solved using algorithms. They may be tedious to implement but are likely to lead to an accurate solution if applicable to a given problem. Computers are likely to use algorithmic problem-solving strategies. Humans are more likely to use rather informal heuristics (e.g., means–ends analysis, working forward, working backward, and generate and test) for solving problems. When ill-structured problems are solved, the choice of an appropriate problem representation powerfully influences the ease of reaching an accurate solution. Additionally, in solving ill-structured problems, people may need to use more than a heuristic or an algorithmic strategy; insight may be required. Many ill-structured problems cannot be solved without the benefit of insight. There are several alternative views of how insightful problem solving takes place. According to the Gestaltist and the neo-Gestaltist views, insightful problem solving is a special process. It comprises more than the sum of its parts and may be evidenced by the suddenness of realizing a solution.

A mental set (also termed entrenchment) is a strategy that has worked in the past but that does not work for a particular problem that needs to be solved in the present. A particular type of mental set is functional fixedness. It involves the inability to see that something that is known to have a particular use also may be used for serving other purposes. Transfer may be either positive or negative. It refers to the carryover of problem-solving skills from one problem or kind of problem to another. Positive transfer across isomorphic problems rarely occurs spontaneously, particularly if the problems appear to be different in content or in context. Incubation follows a period of intensive work on a problem. It involves laying a problem to rest for a while and then returning to it. In this way, subconscious work can continue on the problem while the problem is consciously ignored.

Experts differ from novices in both the amount and the organization of knowledge that they bring to bear on problem solving in the domain of their expertise. For experts, many aspects of problem solving may be governed by automatic processes. Such automaticity usually facilitates the expert's ability to solve problems in the given area of expertise. When problems involve novel elements requiring novel strategies, however, the automaticity of some procedures actually may impede problem solving, at least temporarily. Expertise in a given domain is viewed mostly from the practice-makes-perfect perspective. However, talent should not be ignored and probably contributes much to the differences among experts.

Creativity involves producing something that is both original and worthwhile. Several factors characterize highly creative individuals. One is extremely high motivation to be creative in a particular field of endeavor (e.g., for the sheer enjoyment of the creative process).A second factor is both non-conformity in violating any conventions that might inhibit the creative work and dedication in maintaining standards of excellence and self-discipline related to the creative work. A third factor in creativity is deep belief in the value of the creative work, as well as willingness to criticize and improve the work. A fourth is careful choice of the problems or subjects on which to focus creative attention. A fifth characteristic of creativity is thought processes characterized by both insight and divergent thinking. A sixth factor is risk taking. The final two factors in creativity are extensive knowledge of the relevant domain and profound commitment to the creative endeavor. In addition, the historical context and the domain and field of endeavor influence the expression of creativity.

Chapter 10 Main Principles of Cognitive Behavioral Therapy

While cognitive biology started the development in 1960s, many appliances of it appeared. **Cognitive behavioral therapy (CBT)** is a psychosocial intervention that is the most widely used evidence-based practice for treating mental disorders. Guided by empirical research, CBT focuses on the development of personal coping strategies that target solving current problems and changing unhelpful patterns in cognitions (e.g., thoughts, beliefs, and attitudes), behaviors, and emotional regulation. It was originally designed to treat depression, and is now used for a number of mental health conditions. In a nutshell, the cognitive model proposes that dysfunctional thinking (which influences the patient's mood and behavior) is common to all psychological disturbances. When people learn to evaluate their thinking in a more realistic and adaptive way, they experience improvement in their emotional state and in their behavior. For example, if you were quite depressed and bounced some checks, you might have an automatic thought, an idea that just seemed to pop up in your mind: "I can't do anything right." This thought might then lead to a particular reaction: you might feel sad (emotion) and retreat to bed (behavior). If you then examined the validity of this idea, you might conclude that you had overgeneralized and that, in fact, you actually do many things well. Looking at your experience from this new perspective would probably make you feel better and lead to more functional behavior. For lasting improvement in patients' mood and behavior, cognitive therapists work at a deeper level of cognition: patients' basic beliefs about themselves, their world, and other people. Modification of their underlying dysfunctional beliefs produces more enduring change. For example, if you continually underestimate your abilities, you might have an underlying belief of incompetence. Modifying this general belief (i.e., seeing yourself in a more realistic light as having both strengthsand weaknesses) can alter your perception of specific situations that you encounter daily. You will no longer have as many thoughts with the theme, "I can't do anything right." Instead, in specific situations where you make mistakes, you will probably think, "I'm not good at this."

The basic principles of cognitive behavior therapy are as follows:

Principle No. 1. Cognitive behavior therapy is based on an ever-evolving formulation of patients' problems and an individual conceptualization of each patient in cognitive terms.

Principle No. 2. Cognitive behavior therapy requires a sound therapeutic alliance.

Principle No. 3. Cognitive behavior therapy emphasizes collaboration and active participation.

Principle No. 4. Cognitive behavior therapy is goal oriented and problem focused.

Principle No. 5. Cognitive behavior therapy initially emphasizes the present.

Principle No. 6. Cognitive behavior therapy is educative, aims to teach the patient to be her own therapist, and emphasizes relapse prevention.

Principle No. 7. Cognitive behavior therapy aims to be time limited.

Principle No. 8. Cognitive behavior therapy sessions are structured. No matter what the diagnosis or stage of treatment, following a certain structure in each session maximizes efficiency and effectiveness. This structure includes an introductory part (doing a mood check, briefly reviewing the week, collaboratively setting an agenda for the session), a middle part (reviewing homework, discussing problems on the agenda, setting new homework, summarizing), and a final part (eliciting feedback). Following this format makes the process of therapy more understandable to patients and increases the likelihood that they will be able to do self-therapy after termination.

Principle No. 9. Cognitive behavior therapy teaches patients to identify, evaluate, and respond to their dysfunctional thoughts and beliefs.

Principle No. 10. Cognitive behavior therapy uses a variety of techniques to change thinking, mood, and behavior. Although cognitive strategies such as Socratic questioning and guided discovery are central to cognitive behavior therapy, behavioral and problem-solving techniques are essential, as are techniques from other orientations that are implemented within a cognitive framework. These basic principles apply to all patients. Therapy does, however, vary considerably according to individual patients, the nature of their difficulties, and their stage of life, as well as their developmental and intellectual level, gender, and cultural background. Treatment also varies depending on patients' goals, their ability to form a strong therapeutic bond, their motivation to change, their previous experience with therapy, and their preferences for treatment, among other factors. The emphasis in treatment also depends on the patient's particular disorder(s). Cognitive behavior therapy for panic disorder involves testing the patient's catastrophic misinterpretations (usually life- or sanity-threatening erroneous predictions) of bodily or mental sensations (Clark, 1989). Anorexia requires a modification of beliefs about personal worth and control (Garner & Bemis, 1985). Substance abuse treatment focuses on negative beliefs about the self and facilitating or permission-granting beliefs about substance use (Beck, Wright, Newman, & Liese, 1993).

Researchers have found that other *bona fide* therapeutic interventions were equally effective for treating certain conditions in adults, but CBT was found to be superior in treating most disorders. Along with interpersonal psychotherapy (IPT), CBT is recommended in treatment guidelines as a psychosocial treatment of choice, and CBT and IPT are the only psychosocial interventions that psychiatry residents are mandated to be trained in.

Printed in Great Britain
by Amazon